This boo~~k belongs t~~o

D1624500

Published by Ladybird Books Ltd
A Penguin Company
Penguin Books Ltd, 80 Strand, London WC2R 0RL, UK
Penguin Books Australia Ltd, Camberwell, Victoria, Australia
Penguin Books (NZ) Ltd, Cnr Airbourne and Rosedale Roads, Albany, Auckland, 1310, New Zealand

1 3 5 7 9 10 8 6 4 2

© LADYBIRD BOOKS MMV

Printed in Italy

Mummies

written by Jillian Powell
illustrated by Jim Eldridge

Ladybird

This is a mummy from Ancient Egypt.

It is thousands of years old.

It has the body of a dead king inside it.

7

The body of the dead king
was wrapped in linen.

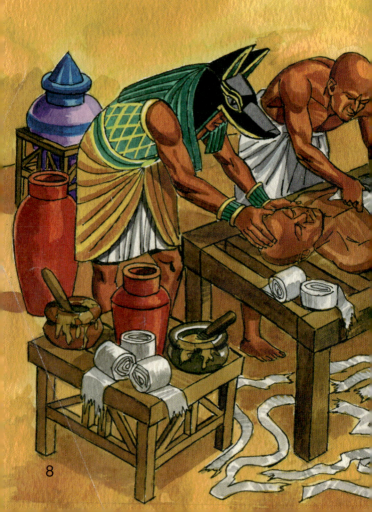

The body was
dried and
perfumed.

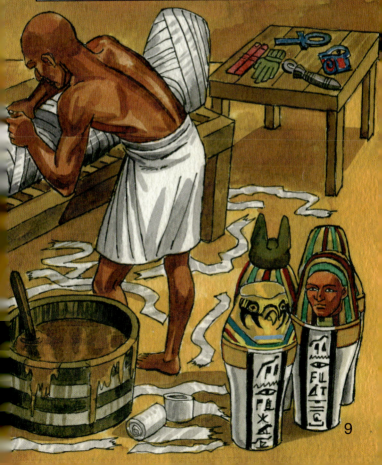

These are lucky charms.

They were wrapped in the linen with the body.

This is the mummy mask.

It went over the mummy's head.

The mask was made to look like the dead king.

mummy mask

The mask of the dead king was made in gold.

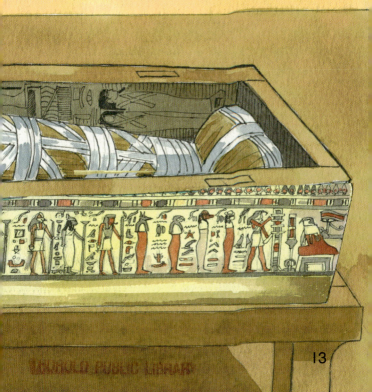

This is the mummy case.

It had pictures painted on the outside.

The mummy was put inside it.

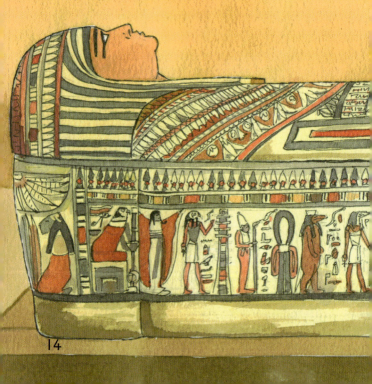

The Egyptians painted magic spells to look after the dead king.

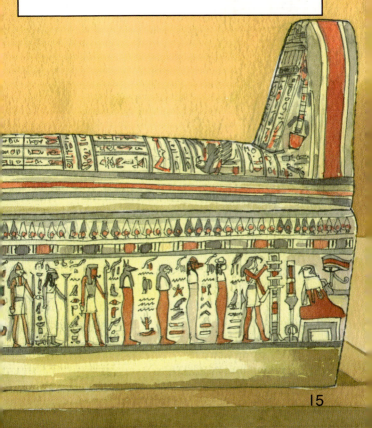

This is the pyramid.

Pyramids were tombs for dead kings.

The mummy case was put inside it.

pyramid

17

This is the sarcophagus.

The mummy case was put inside it.

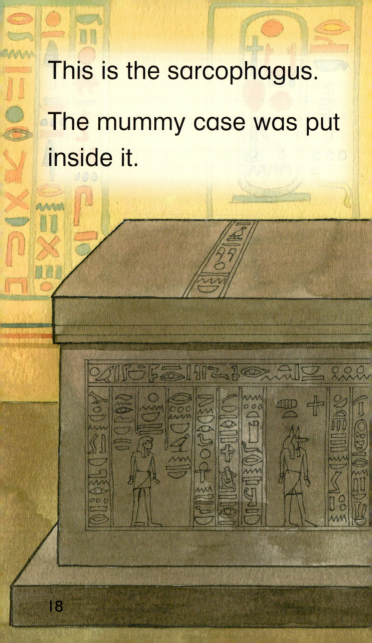

The sarcophagus was a
coffin made of stone.
It was inside the pyramid.

This is the burial chamber.

It was inside the pyramid.

sarcophagus

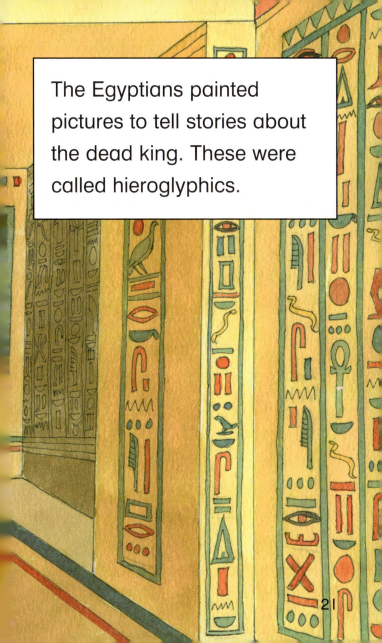

The Egyptians painted pictures to tell stories about the dead king. These were called hieroglyphics.

These are canopic jars.

They were put inside the burial chamber.

The canopic jars had the dead king's body parts inside them.

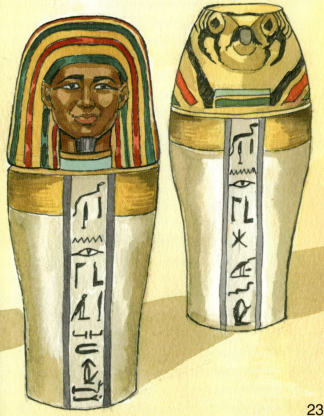

These are models of
servants.

They were put inside the
burial chamber.

The king wanted servants to help him in his next life.

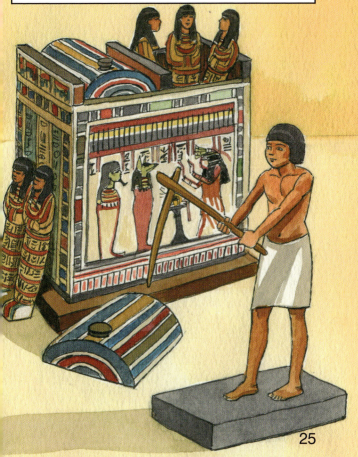

This is a famous mummy.

It is the mummy of the boy king Tutankhamun.

Tutankhamun lived more than three thousand years ago.

Can you remember how a mummy was made?

mummy

mummy mask

mummy case

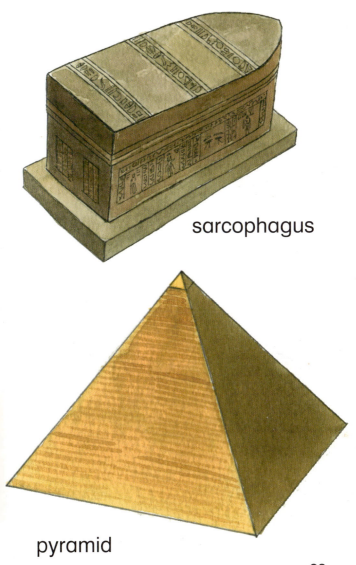

sarcophagus

pyramid

29

Index